D0764019

1A
Yreka:
2-13-09
Mt. Shasta:
8-28-09

Etna:
12-3-09

Dunsmuir:
4-16-10

McCloud:
10-16-10

Yreka

_____

HOW TO DRAW
CARS

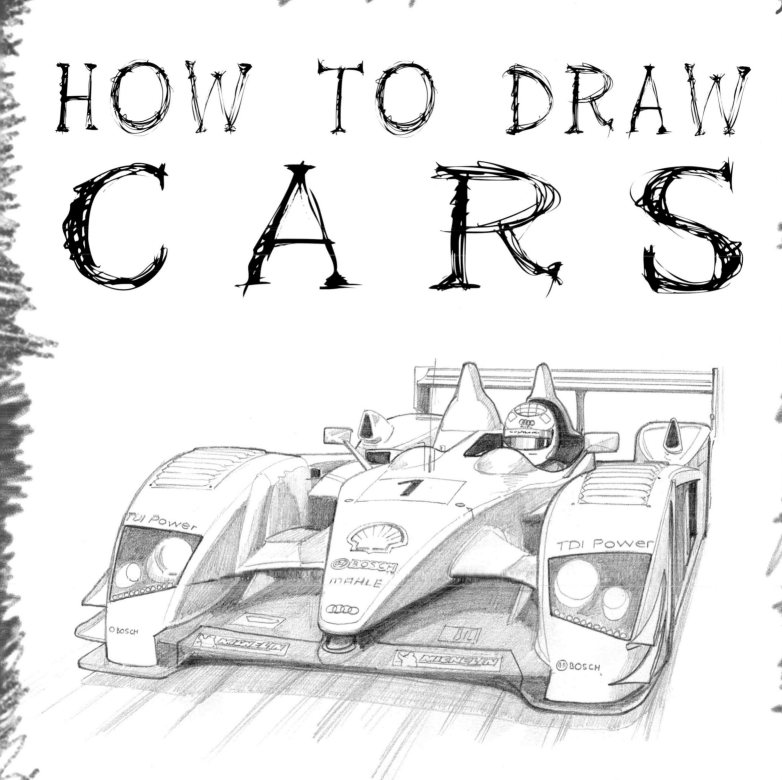

Mark Bergin

PowerKiDS
press

New York

Published in 2009 by The Rosen Publishing Group, Inc.
29 East 21st Street, New York, NY 10010

Editor: Rob Walker
U.S. Editor: Kara Murray

Library of Congress Cataloging-in-Publication Data

Bergin, Mark.
  Cars / Mark Bergin.
      p. cm. — (How to draw)
  Includes index.
  ISBN 978-1-4358-2520-8 (library binding)
ISBN 978-1-4358-2649-6 (pbk)
ISBN 978-1-4358-2661-8 (6-pack)
  1. Drawing—Technique—Juvenile literature. 2. Automobiles in
art—Juvenile literature. I. Title. II. Title: Cars.
  NC825.A8B47 2009
  743'.89629222—dc22

                                              2007047938

Manufactured in China

Contents

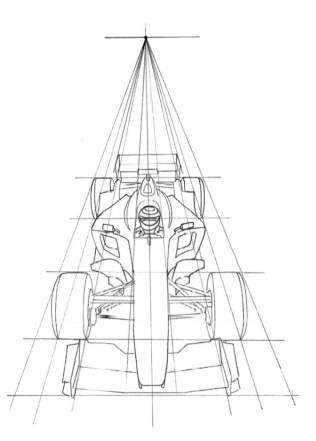

Making a Start

Learning to draw is about looking and seeing. Keep practicing and get to know your subject. Use a sketchbook to make quick sketches. Start by doodling, and experiment with shapes and patterns. There are many ways to draw, this book shows one method. Visit art galleries, look at artists' drawings, see how friends draw, and most importantly, find your own way.

Audi R10

Remember that practice will make a drawing work.
If it looks wrong, start again. Keep working at it —
the more you draw, the more you will learn.

Subaru Impreza STI

Honda S2000

Saleen S7

Perspective

If you look at a car from different viewpoints, you will see that the part of the car that is closest to you will look larger, and the part farthest away from you will look smaller. Drawing in perspective is a way of creating a feeling of space and three dimensions on a flat surface.

(Below) This drawing has a single high vanishing point. From this viewpoint the car looks as if it is zooming out toward you.

V.P. = vanishing point

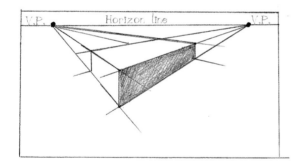

(Above) A car's basic shape is like a rectangular box. Most car drawings can start with this type of shape.

(Right) Note how the construction lines get wider apart as they get closer to you. Toward the back of the car, the lines are closer together because it is farther away from you.

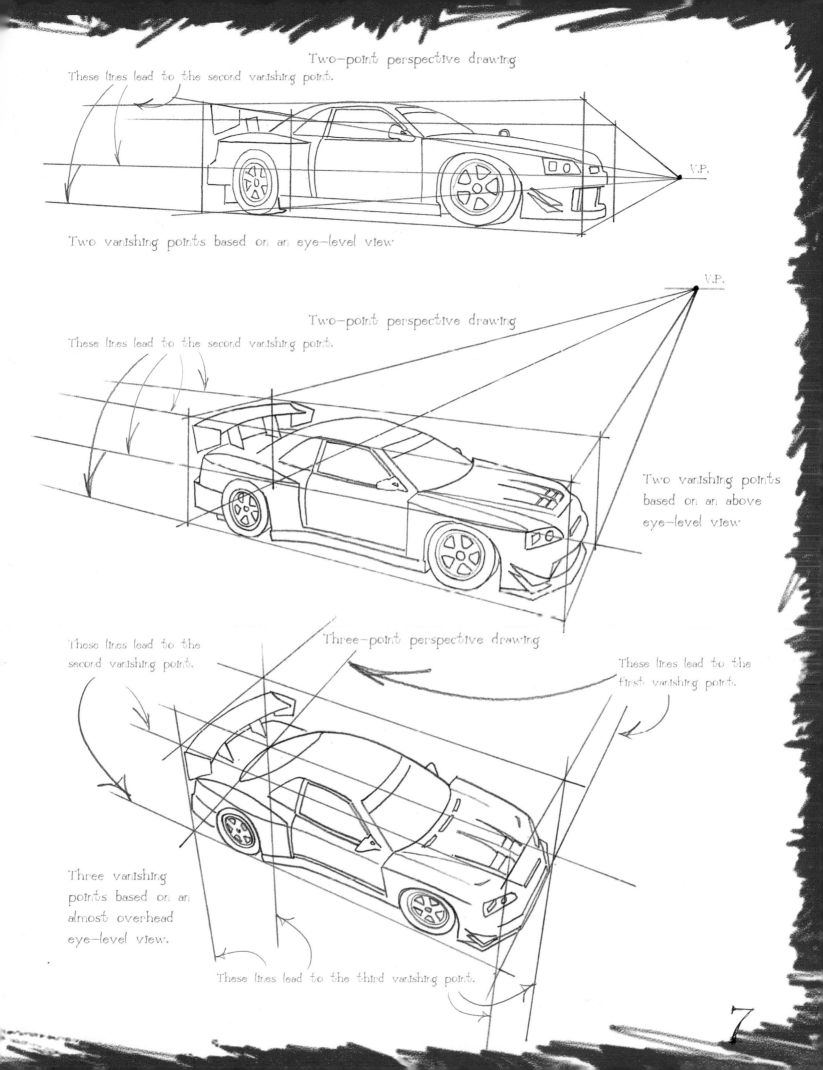

Two-point perspective drawing

These lines lead to the second vanishing point.

V.P.

Two vanishing points based on an eye-level view

V.P.

Two-point perspective drawing

These lines lead to the second vanishing point.

Two vanishing points based on an above eye-level view

Three-point perspective drawing

These lines lead to the second vanishing point.

These lines lead to the first vanishing point.

Three vanishing points based on an almost overhead eye-level view.

These lines lead to the third vanishing point.

7

Photographs

Drawing from a photograph can help you practice your drawing skills. It is important that you consider the position of your drawing on the paper. This is called composition.

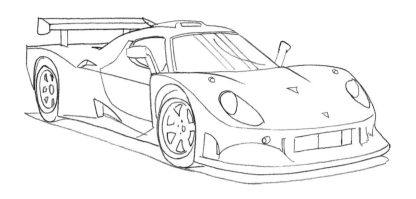

Grids

(Above) Make a tracing of the photograph and draw a grid over it.

(Above) Lightly draw another grid in the same proportions on your drawing paper. You can now transfer the shapes from your tracing to your drawing paper using these grids as a guide. This method is called squaring up.

Mid-toned area

Darkest tone

Shadow on road surface

(Above) A photograph is flat. To make your drawing appear more three-dimensional, look at which side the light is coming from so that you can put in areas of shadow.

(Below) Add more tone and detail to finish the drawing.

Shiny surfaces reflect light, leave these areas white.

Add in background to give atmosphere to your drawing.

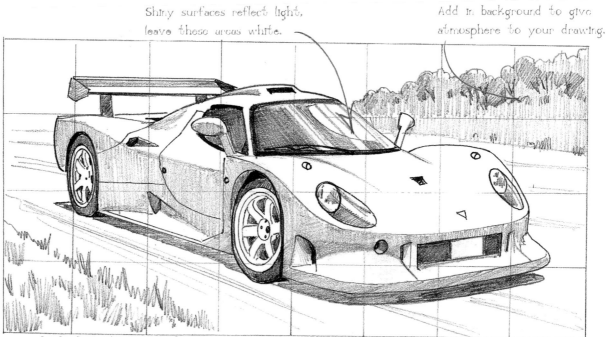

Add texture and shadow to your drawing.

Materials

Try using different types of drawing papers and materials. Experiment with charcoal, wax crayons, and pastels. All pens, from felt—tips to ballpoints, will make interesting marks, or try drawing with pen and ink on wet paper.

Hard **pencils** are grayer and soft pencils are blacker. Pencils are graded from #1 (the softest) to #4 (the hardest).

Charcoal is very soft and can be used for big, bold drawings. Spray charcoal drawings with fixative to prevent further smudging.

Fixative is a type of resin that is sprayed over a finished drawing to prevent smudging. Fixatives should be used under adult supervision.

Pastels are even softer than charcoal and come in a wide range of colors. Spray pastel drawings with fixative too to prevent further smudging.

Create special effects by scraping away parts of a drawing done with **wax crayons.**

Lines drawn in ink cannot be erased so keep your ink drawings sketchy and less rigid. Don't worry about mistakes as these can be lost in the drawing as it develops.

Silhouette

Swift

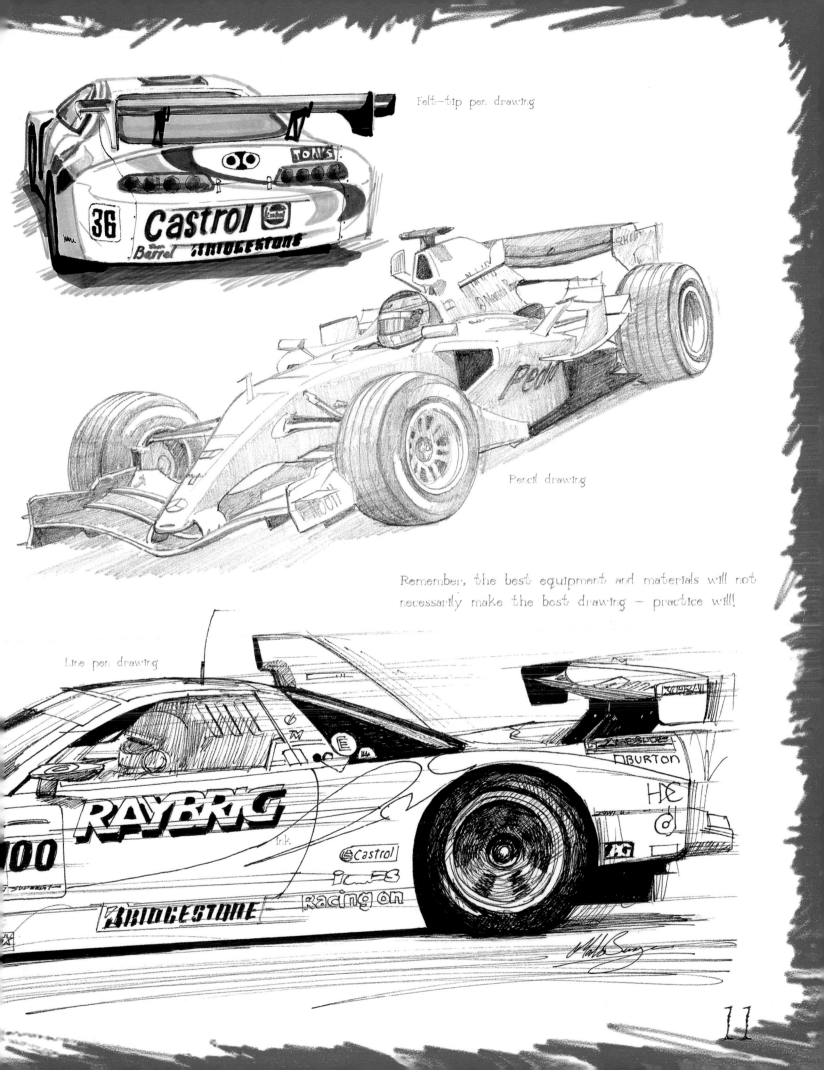

Felt-tip pen drawing

Pencil drawing

Remember, the best equipment and materials will not necessarily make the best drawing — practice will!

Line pen drawing

Sketching

You can't always rely on your memory, so you have to look around and find real—life things you want to draw. Using a sketchbook is one of the best ways to build up drawing skills. Learn to observe objects: see how they move, how they are made, and how they work. What you draw should be what you have seen. Since the 15th century, artists have used sketchbooks to record their ideas and drawings.

Sketching models

Try drawing model cars. It is good practice for seeing and observing.

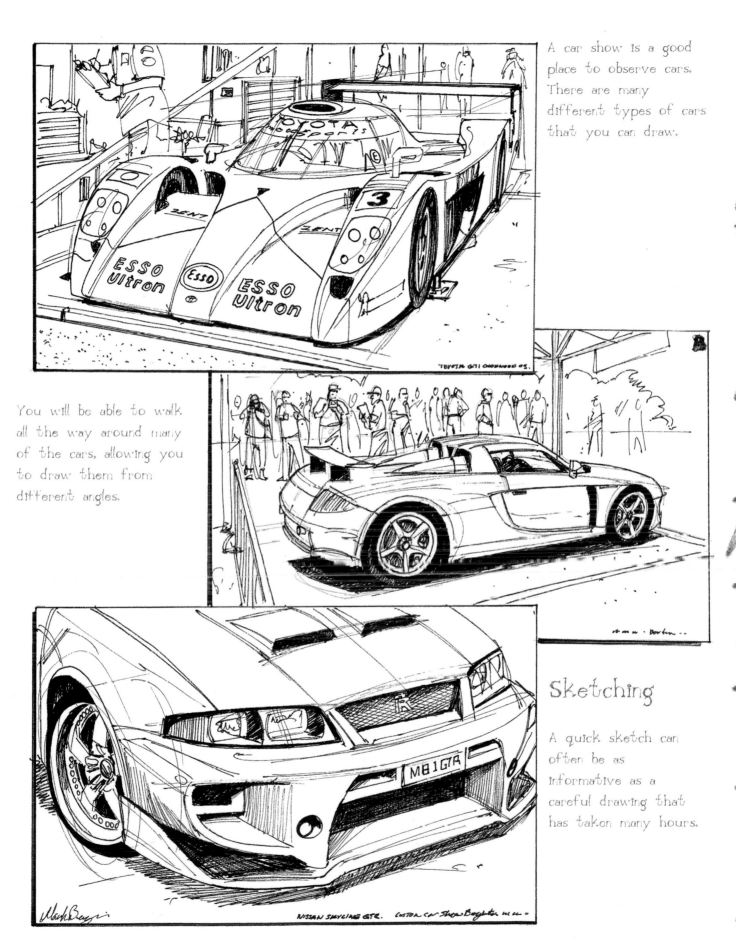

A car show is a good place to observe cars. There are many different types of cars that you can draw.

You will be able to walk all the way around many of the cars, allowing you to draw them from different angles.

Sketching

A quick sketch can often be as informative as a careful drawing that has taken many hours.

Honda Civic R

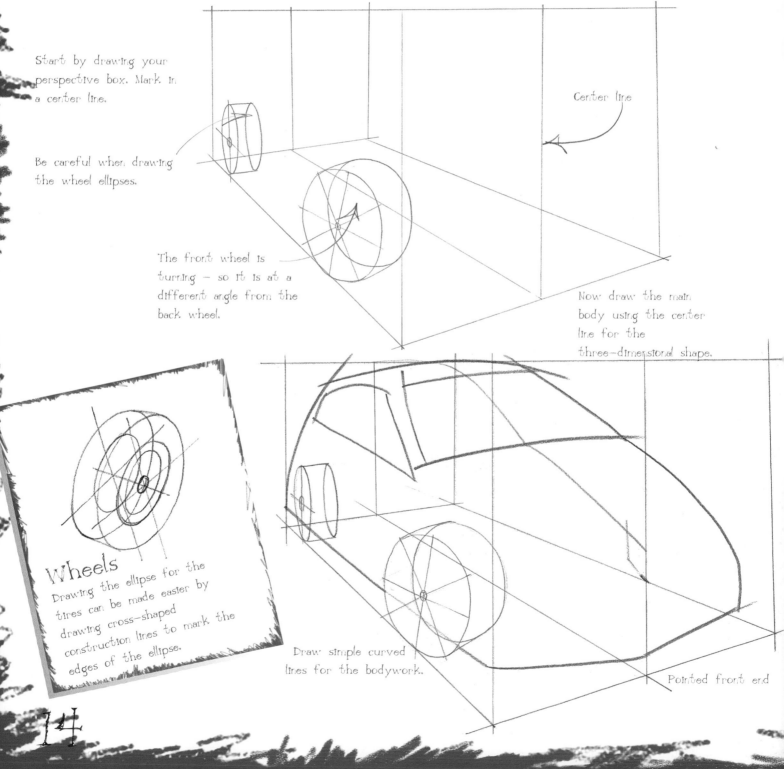

The Honda Civic R can be customized to a driver's specifications. The addition of chrome wheels, air intakes, skirt, and a powerful engine can transform this car into an urban street racer.

Start by drawing your perspective box. Mark in a center line.

Be careful when drawing the wheel ellipses.

The front wheel is turning – so it is at a different angle from the back wheel.

Center line

Now draw the main body using the center line for the three-dimensional shape.

Wheels
Drawing the ellipse for the tires can be made easier by drawing cross–shaped construction lines to mark the edges of the ellipse.

Draw simple curved lines for the bodywork.

Pointed front end

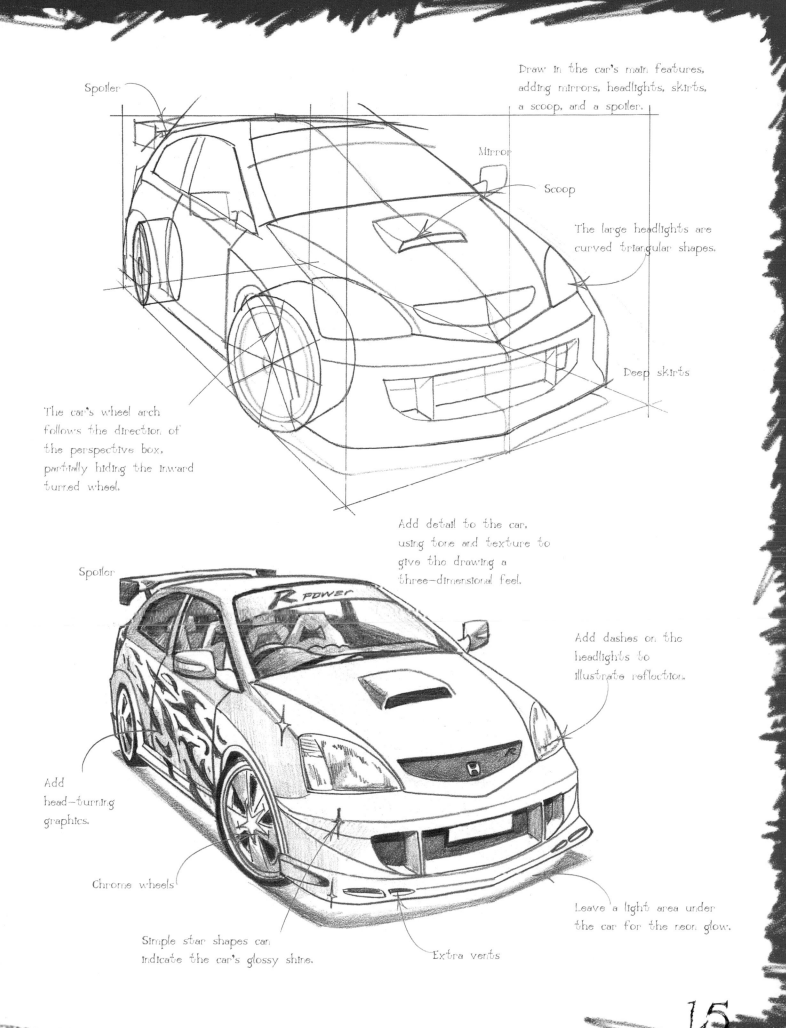

Draw in the car's main features,
adding mirrors, headlights, skirts,
a scoop, and a spoiler.

Spoiler

Mirror

Scoop

The large headlights are
curved triangular shapes.

Deep skirts

The car's wheel arch
follows the direction of
the perspective box,
partially hiding the inward
turned wheel.

Add detail to the car,
using tone and texture to
give the drawing a
three-dimensional feel.

Spoiler

R power

Add dashes on the
headlights to
illustrate reflection.

Add
head-turning
graphics.

Chrome wheels

Simple star shapes can
indicate the car's glossy shine.

Extra vents

Leave a light area under
the car for the neon glow.

15

Aston Martin DBS

The new Aston Martin DBS is James Bond's car in the 2006 film *Casino Royale*. Its style and power have made it a British classic.

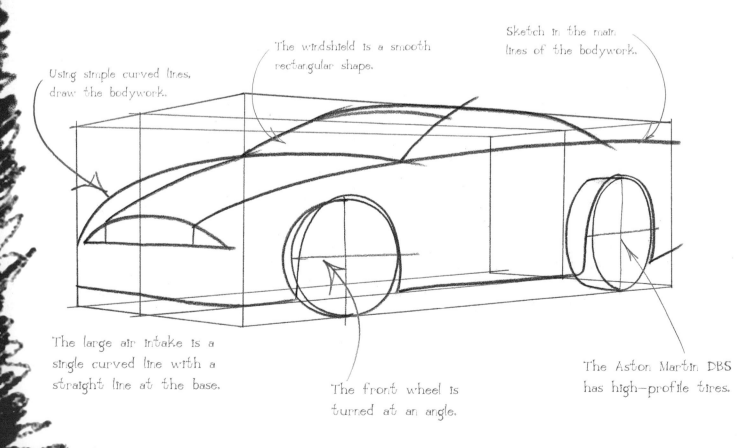

Start by drawing a simple perspective box with a center line.

Sketch in the main lines of the bodywork.

The windshield is a smooth rectangular shape.

Using simple curved lines, draw the bodywork.

The large air intake is a single curved line with a straight line at the base.

The front wheel is turned at an angle.

The Aston Martin DBS has high-profile tires.

Draw in the main features of the car, adding mirrors, windows, headlights, doors, and skirts.

Composition

Use different shapes to frame your composition. This can improve your drawing.

Draw the air intake in the skirts using straight lines.

Add lines for the door, note how they curve in at the top to follow the shape of the bodywork.

Draw in the small rear end of the car using a series of curved lines.

Don't forget to draw in parts like the door pillar on the far side.

Now add the final details to the car.

AM DBS

Darken areas where the light would not reach.

Divide the wheel into triangular sections and add detail for the large alloy wheels.

Add tone to the bodywork to give it a three-dimensional look.

17

Ford GT

The Ford GT is a redesigned version of the 1960s classic Le Mans winning car, the GT40. This new version is longer and larger than the GT40 and has a supercharged V8 engine.

Start by drawing a simple perspective box with a center line.

Draw in the basic shape of the windows.

Two simple curved lines create the front shape of the car.

Draw ellipses to indicate the wheels.

Two long curved lines will create the lower front part of the car.

Add the main features of the car: air intakes, headlights, and side mirrors.

You can use profile drawings or photographs to help you with size and proportion. They can be a great help for the detail of wheels and air intakes.

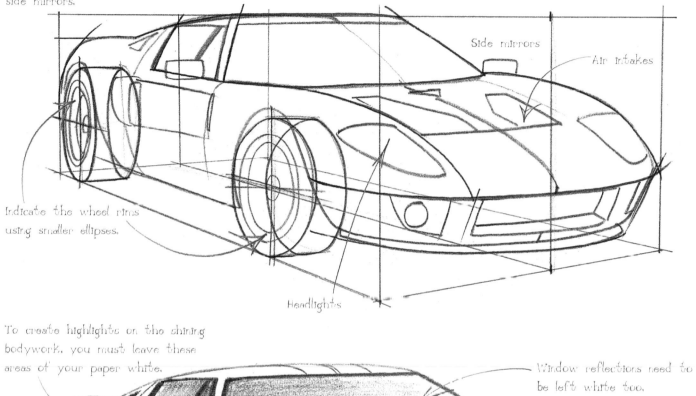

Side mirrors

Air intakes

Indicate the wheel rims using smaller ellipses.

Headlights

To create highlights on the shining bodywork, you must leave these areas of your paper white.

Window reflections need to be left white too.

Darken areas of your drawing where the light would not reach.

Remove any construction lines.

Add the Ford double stripes.

Subaru Impreza

The Subaru Impreza is one of the most successful modern rally cars with its 4-wheel drive and turbocharged engine. The Norwegian Petter Solberg won the world rally championship in this car in 2003.

Start by drawing a simple perspective box with a center line.

Sketch in the wheels with ellipses.

Add the car's basic body shape.

Draw in a simple rectangular shape for the windshield and the roof.

Use curved lines to draw in the front of the car.

The front of the car is curved.

Draw in the wheel arches.

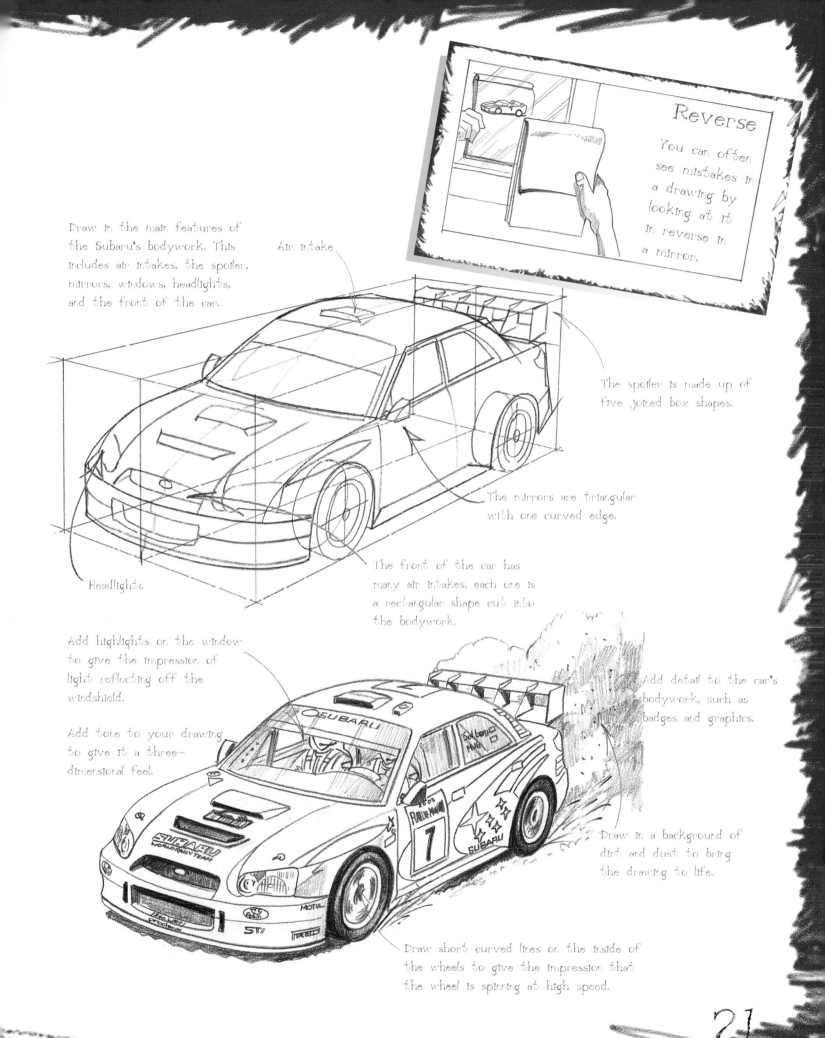

Draw in the main features of the Subaru's bodywork. This includes air intakes, the spoiler, mirrors, windows, headlights, and the front of the car.

Air intake

Reverse

You can often see mistakes in a drawing by looking at it in reverse in a mirror.

The spoiler is made up of five joined box shapes.

The mirrors are triangular with one curved edge.

Headlights

The front of the car has many air intakes, each one is a rectangular shape cut into the bodywork.

Add highlights on the window to give the impression of light reflecting off the windshield.

Add tone to your drawing to give it a three-dimensional feel.

Add detail to the car's bodywork, such as badges and graphics.

Draw in a background of dirt and dust to bring the drawing to life.

Draw short curved lines on the inside of the wheels to give the impression that the wheel is spinning at high speed.

21

NASCAR

NASCAR (National Association for Stock Car Auto Racing) races cars on oval tracks like Daytona. Its banked corners make it one of the most exciting and colorful experiences in motor sports. Cars can average speeds of 200 miles per hour (320 km/h) as they pass close to one another.

Start your drawing with a simple perspective box with a center line.

Draw in ellipses to indicate the position of the wheels.

Draw in the main bodywork.

Simple rectangular shapes can be used to draw the front windshield and the roof.

The car hood is very long. Use long, curved lines to draw it.

The rear of the car is quite angular so use straight lines to draw it.

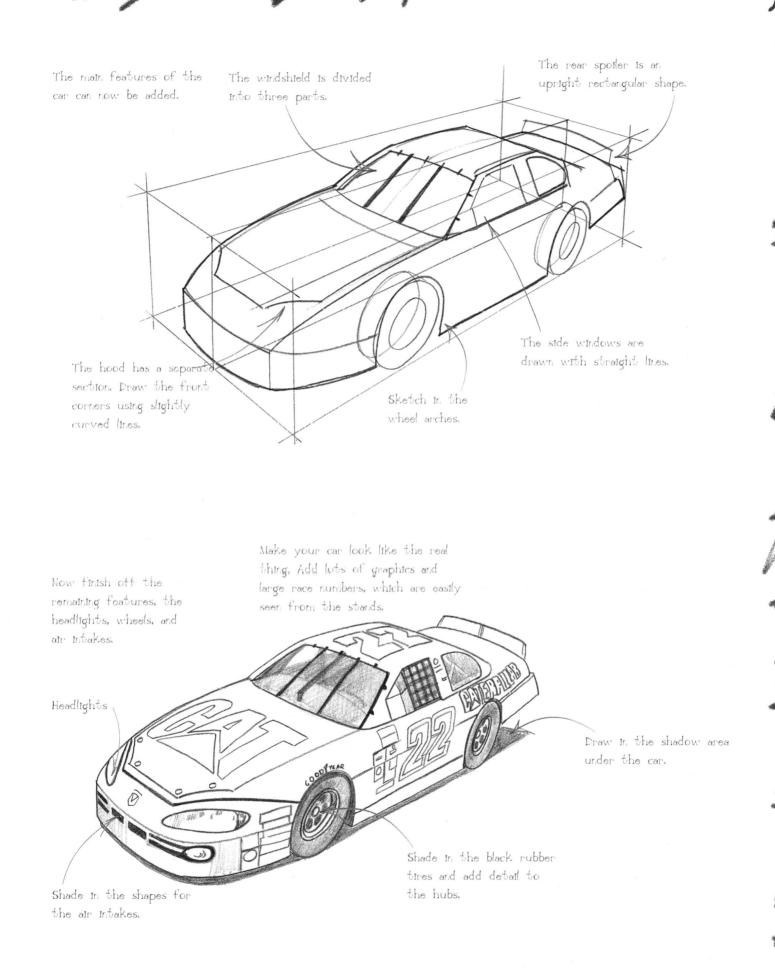

The main features of the car can now be added.

The windshield is divided into three parts.

The rear spoiler is an upright rectangular shape.

The hood has a separate section. Draw the front corners using slightly curved lines.

Sketch in the wheel arches.

The side windows are drawn with straight lines.

Now finish off the remaining features, the headlights, wheels, and air intakes.

Make your car look like the real thing. Add lots of graphics and large race numbers, which are easily seen from the stands.

Headlights

Draw in the shadow area under the car.

Shade in the shapes for the air intakes.

Shade in the black rubber tires and add detail to the hubs.

23

Bentley Speed 8

The Bentley Speed 8 won the Le Mans 24-hour race in 2003. In this event it covered 3,197 miles (5,145 km) at an average speed of 133 miles per hour (214 km/h).

First draw a perspective box. Remember this car is quite low, so make the box low too.

Draw in the center line.

The main car body takes up the lower half of this box.

Sketch the basic shape of the car. Draw an oval canopy on the center line.

Using curved lines, draw in the pointed front end of the car.

Draw in two curved wheel arches at the front of the car.

Now sketch in the main features: wing mirrors, headlights, spoiler, wheels, air intakes, and windshield.

The windshield takes up the front of the canopy. Use the center line to help mark its position.

The spoiler is as high as the roof on this car. Use the construction lines to indicate its position.

The headlights are just a simple oval shape.

The wing mirrors are cone shaped.

The wheels can be marked using thin ellipses.

Sketching curved lines here allows the box shapes at the front of the car to become air intakes.

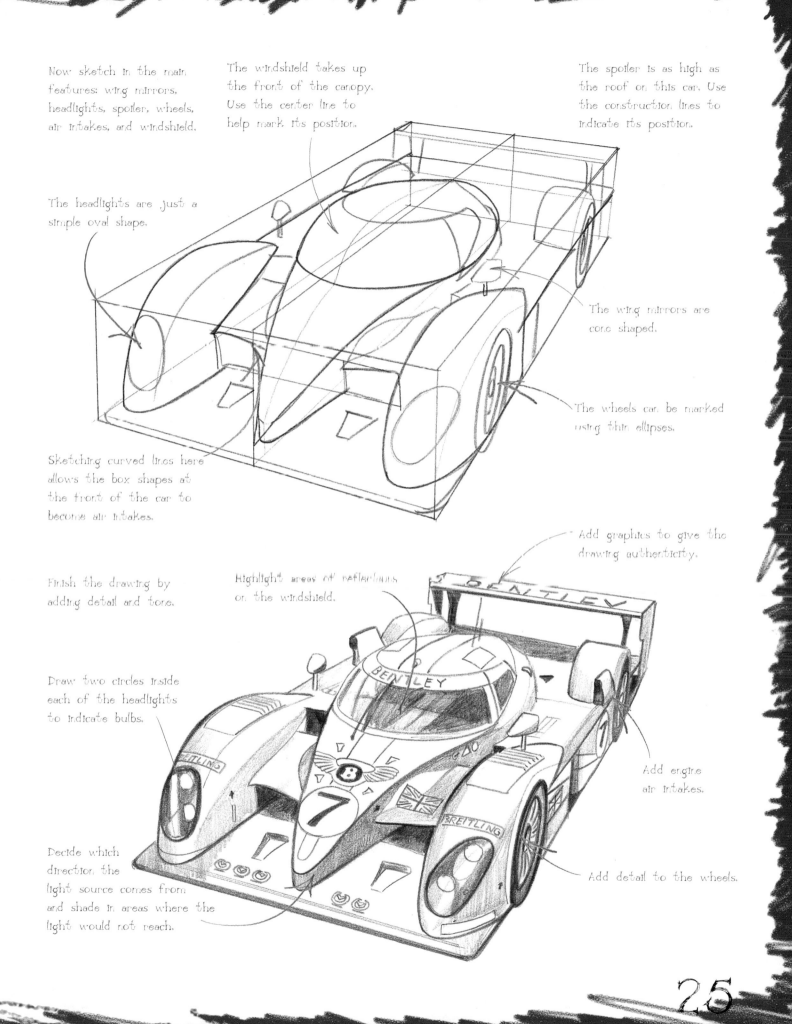

Add graphics to give the drawing authenticity.

Finish the drawing by adding detail and tone.

Highlight areas of reflections on the windshield.

Draw two circles inside each of the headlights to indicate bulbs.

Add engine air intakes.

Decide which direction the light source comes from and shade in areas where the light would not reach.

Add detail to the wheels.

25

Ferrari FXX

The Ferrari FXX is a recent Italian supercar. It is a Ferrari Enzo that has been tuned up and reworked to make it the ultimate race car. Its 12-cylinder engine propels this super light car, it weighs 2,546 pounds (1,155 kg), to a speed of almost 200 miles per hour (320 km/h)!

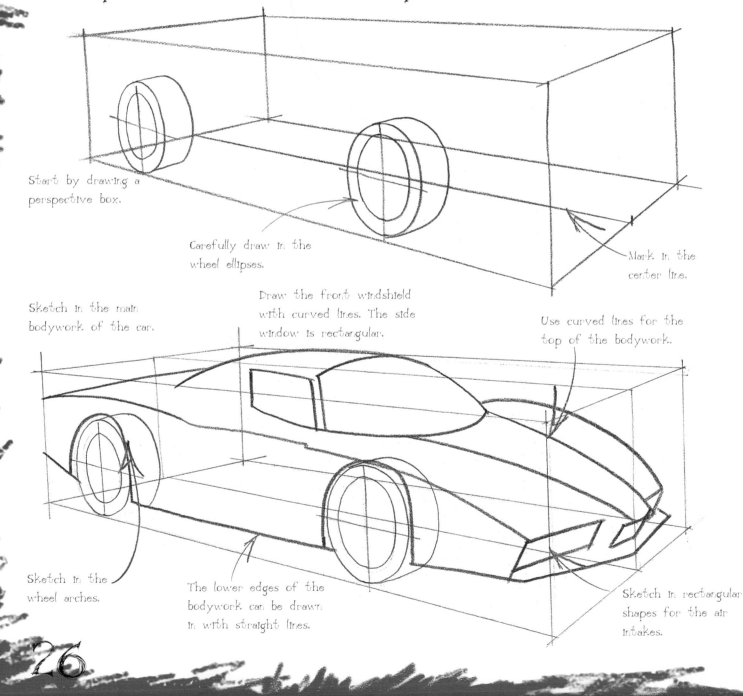

Start by drawing a perspective box.

Carefully draw in the wheel ellipses.

Mark in the center line.

Sketch in the main bodywork of the car.

Draw the front windshield with curved lines. The side window is rectangular.

Use curved lines for the top of the bodywork.

Sketch in the wheel arches.

The lower edges of the bodywork can be drawn in with straight lines.

Sketch in rectangular shapes for the air intakes.

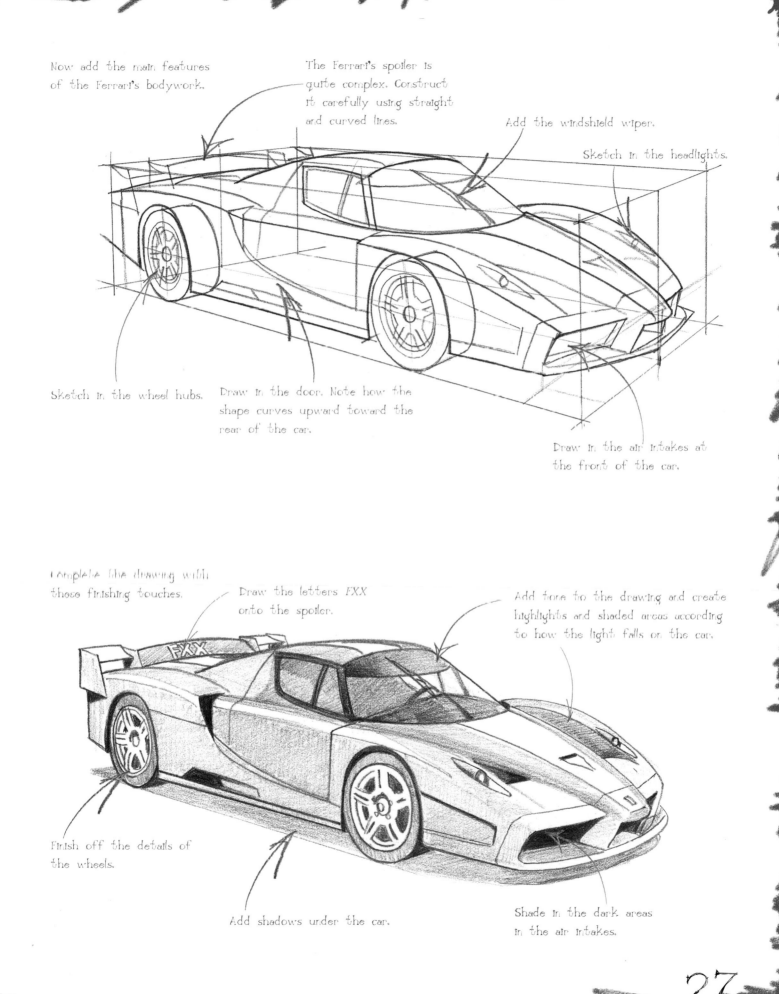

Now add the main features
of the Ferrari's bodywork.

The Ferrari's spoiler is
quite complex. Construct
it carefully using straight
and curved lines.

Add the windshield wiper.

Sketch in the headlights.

Sketch in the wheel hubs.

Draw in the door. Note how the
shape curves upward toward the
rear of the car.

Draw in the air intakes at
the front of the car.

Complete the drawing with
these finishing touches.

Draw the letters FXX
onto the spoiler.

Add tone to the drawing and create
highlights and shaded areas according
to how the light falls on the car.

Finish off the details of
the wheels.

Add shadows under the car.

Shade in the dark areas
in the air intakes.

Ferrari F1

Michael Schumacher won many races in Formula 1 driving the Ferrari F1. It can reach speeds of 224 miles per hour (360 km/h). The car's shape gives it a strong downforce, which helps keep it on the road.

Start the drawing with a perspective box with a center line.

Draw in four wheels as they can all be seen on the Ferrari F1.

Draw in the main bodywork of the car.

The car is in three main sections: the rear end, the cockpit, and the nose.

Join both sets of wheels with axlelike construction lines. This will make it easier to place the main body of the car into the drawing.

Rear end

Draw the cockpit with a square front and long, curved lines.

Extend the long, curved lines of the cockpit to draw in the rounded nose of the car.

The rear end has a flat front and curves inward toward the back end of the car.

Nose

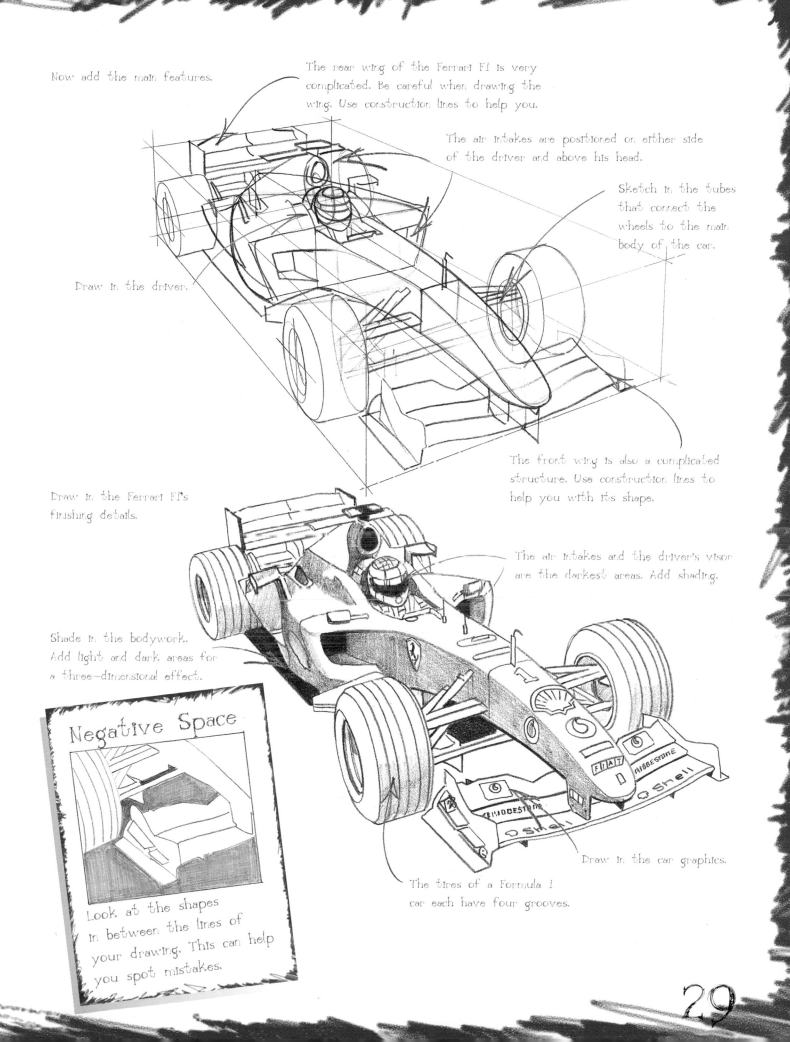

Now add the main features.

The rear wing of the Ferrari F1 is very complicated. Be careful when drawing the wing. Use construction lines to help you.

The air intakes are positioned on either side of the driver and above his head.

Sketch in the tubes that connect the wheels to the main body of the car.

Draw in the driver.

The front wing is also a complicated structure. Use construction lines to help you with its shape.

Draw in the Ferrari F1's finishing details.

The air intakes and the driver's visor are the darkest areas. Add shading.

Shade in the bodywork. Add light and dark areas for a three-dimensional effect.

Negative Space

Look at the shapes in between the lines of your drawing. This can help you spot mistakes.

The tires of a Formula 1 car each have four grooves.

Draw in the car graphics.

Thrust SSC

The Thrust SSC set the new land speed record on October 15, 1997, at Black Rock Desert, Nevada. Its 110,000 horsepower jet engines propelled the driver, Andy Green, to more than 763 miles per hour (1,228 km/h) to make it the world's first supersonic land speed record.

First draw a long perspective box.

Start to draw in the jet engines on each side.

For each engine draw two ellipses, the rear one smaller than the front one. Then connect them with straight lines.

Mark in the center line.

Add a triangle at the rear to form the car's fin.

Draw in the front part of each engine. Draw two smaller ellipses, one inside the other, and join them to the body of the engine with curved lines.

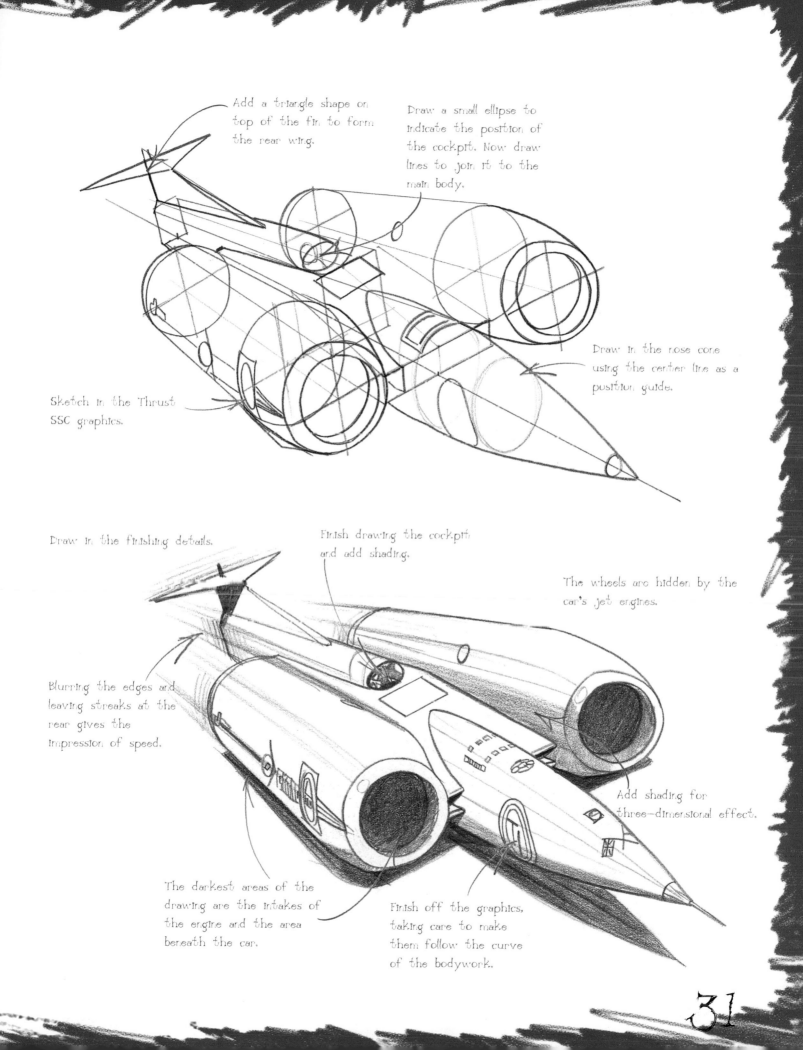

Add a triangle shape on top of the fin to form the rear wing.

Draw a small ellipse to indicate the position of the cockpit. Now draw lines to join it to the main body.

Draw in the nose cone using the center line as a position guide.

Sketch in the Thrust SSC graphics.

Draw in the finishing details.

Finish drawing the cockpit and add shading.

The wheels are hidden by the car's jet engines.

Blurring the edges and leaving streaks at the rear gives the impression of speed.

Add shading for three-dimensional effect.

The darkest areas of the drawing are the intakes of the engine and the area beneath the car.

Finish off the graphics, taking care to make them follow the curve of the bodywork.

Glossary

composition (kom-puh-ZIH-shun) The positioning of a subject on the drawing paper.

construction lines (kun-STRUK-shun LYNZ) Structural lines used in the early stages of a drawing.

light source (LYT SORS) The direction that light is coming from.

proportion (pruh-POR-shun) The correct relationship of scale between each part of a drawing.

rigid (RIH-jid) Stiff.

sketchbook (SKECH-buk) A book for drawing sketches, or quick drawings.

squaring up (SKWER-ing UP) Transferring a drawing accurately using square grids.

texture (TEKS-chur) How something feels or looks.

three-dimensional (three-deh-MENCH-nul) The effect of making an image look lifelike or real rather than flat.

vanishing point (VA-nish-ing POYNT) A point in a perspective drawing where parallel lines seem to converge.

Index

Web Sites

Due to the changing nature of Internet links, PowerKids Press has developed an online list of Web sites related to the subject of this book. This site is updated regularly. Please use this link to access the list:
www.powerkidslinks.com/htd/cars/